The World's Best Programmer

Which are the best software development tools, processes, and people skills?

RAHUL SRINIVASAN

Many of the designations used by manufacturers and sellers to distinguish their products are claimed as trademarks, even if not expressly identified in this book.

The author has taken care in the preparation of this book, but makes no expressed or implied warranty of any kind and assumes no responsibility for errors or omissions. No liability is assumed for incidental or consequential damages in connection with or arising out of use of the information or programs contained herein.

First Edition, 2020

Dedication

For Ma.

Disclaimer

This book reflects my personal views on all the topics presented. It does not reflect the views of my employers, colleagues, or other institutions I am affiliated with.

Table of Contents

Introduction

No, I am not the World's Best Programmer, but I am hoping you could be !

I have always believed that the best results can be achieved from a combination of the best technologies, processes, and people.

But, how do you choose the best technology when there is a mind-boggling range to choose from? Which programming language is the best? Which JavaScript framework (a new one seems to be created every day!) is the best? Which people skills should you build to be the best developer?

These are the sea of questions I search for you and me and give the answers.

For the purpose of this search, we will look at tools to build a simple e-commerce site, which is not yet at the scale of an Amazon or a Flipkart. All the tools selected should have the lowest possible cost.

For Part I, I approach the journey, honestly, as a learner, leaving behind pre-conceived ideas. I intend to go where my research pulls me and then present the same without clouding it with my prejudices.

Onward and upward!

How to read this book

There is no fixed sequence. You can pick any chapter at random and start reading.

The target audience for this book are both developers and people looking to build or lead their software teams. Therefore, I have kept this book as non-technical and brief as possible.

For Part I (Technologies), I have divided each chapter into the following sections:

- *Short Answer*: The answer. Upfront. With no nonsense. If you are short on time, you can simply read the *short answer* and skip the entire chapter!

- *Long Answer*: The analysis of how I reached the answer.

- *The Basics*: If you are an experienced programmer, you can skip this section.

- *The Facts*: Statistics from across the Internet to help find the solution.

- *The Winner*: The winner based on the analysis.

- *Thoughts*: Some thoughts on the winner and alternate views. This is not present in every chapter.

Part II (Processes) and Part III (People) do not have these classifications.

PART I

// Technologies //

CHAPTER ONE

WORLD'S BEST

PROGRAMMING LANGUAGE

Short Answer: Python

Long Answer

I expect this question to be the most controversial. During my college days, the battle was on between Java and Visual Basic, and then subsequently Java vs C#. Now, there is an explosion of languages, each with its fervent supporters, so this is indeed a tough topic to navigate!

Conversely, in larger software companies, such as NIIT and TCS, developers may be hired to code in one language, but may work on a multitude of languages and technologies. One month, you will be working on C#, the next month on Tableau, the next month on Python, and so on. This to me, is a very positive trend because of a few reasons:

1. It recognizes software development as a skill. As long as a programmer has development skills, he can transcend and work on multiple languages.

2. Learning newer technologies ensures that the developer is never obsolete. We have so many horror stories of developers working on legacy systems built on ancient technologies. When they lose their job, it is nearly impossible for them to land a new job (on the other hand, if their company is financially secure, these programmers are guaranteed a job for life!)

3. Companies investing in their employees and promoting a learning culture is always a good sign.

The Basics

"The best programs are written so that computing machines can perform them quickly and so that human beings can understand them clearly. A programmer is ideally an essayist who works with traditional aesthetic and literary forms as well as mathematical concepts, to communicate the way that an algorithm works and to convince a reader that the results will be correct."

--- Donald E. Knuth

Computer Scientist, Professor emeritus at Stanford University

Computers do not understand human language. Hence, we have programming languages to "tell" the computer what we want it to do.

Almost all programming languages are written in English. Whether they're programming in HTML, JavaScript, Python, or Ruby, programmers around the world use the same English keywords and syntax in their code. Some non-English programming languages exist but none of these languages are widespread or mainstream.

Jon von Neumann designed the *von Neumann architecture*, where a CPU could execute instructions from RAM and alter data in the same RAM. The von Neumann architecture is the basic premise of almost all modern computers.

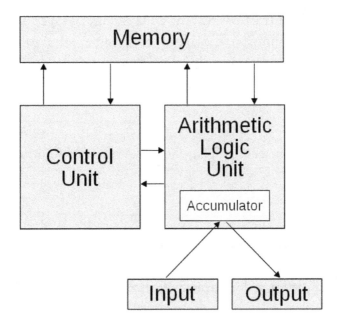

Figure 1: von Neumann Architecture

Stored-program computers can be referred to as *von Neumann architecture machines*. They run programs stored somewhere on the system and are universal i.e. it can run any computable algorithm.

The actual raw instructions that the CPU executes is called *machine code*. A slightly more human readable form of machine code is called *assembly language* and a program called an *assembler* is used to convert the assembly instructions into machine code.

Higher level languages like C or C++ are converted into machine code using a *compiler*.

Programming languages like JavaScript, Python, and Ruby are *interpreted*. For these languages, the interpreter executes the program directly, translating each statement one line at a time into machine code.

Programming languages like C++, COBOL, and Visual Basic are *compiled*. For these languages, after the code is written, a compiler translates all the code into machine code, and an executable file is created.

FORTRAN, developed by IBM in 1954, was the first widely used high-level general purpose programming language to have a functional implementation. It is regarded as the first compiler.

Amazingly, more than a half century later, it is still a popular language for high-performance computing!

Two more 1950s languages that are still in use today are LISP (1958) and COBOL (1959).

More importantly for us, in the 1990s, there was rapid growth in the Internet and this led to a huge number of languages that were developed:

- 1990 – Haskell

- 1990 – Python

- 1991 – Visual Basic

- 1993 – Lua

- 1993 – R

- 1994 – CLOS (part of ANSI Common Lisp)

- 1995 – Ruby

- 1995 – Ada 95

- 1995 – Java

- 1995 – Delphi

- 1995 – JavaScript

- 1995 – PHP

- 1997 – Rebol

It is impossible to cover every single programming language in this book (or, rather, in any book!), so I would suggest reading Wikipedia's mammoth list of programming languages:

https://en.wikipedia.org/wiki/List_of_programming_languages

The Facts

Enough with the basics and anecdotes. Let us see what the data says!

As per PYPL, below is the top ranking for July 2020. The PYPL PopularitY of Programming Language Index is created by **analysing how often language tutorials are searched on Google**.

Worldwide, Jul 2020 compared to a year ago:

Rank	Change	Language	Share	Trend
1		Python	31.73 %	+3.9 %
2		Java	17.13 %	-2.7 %
3		Javascript	7.98 %	-0.3 %
4		C#	6.67 %	-0.6 %
5	↑	C/C++	5.93 %	+0.1 %
6	↓	PHP	5.64 %	-1.1 %
7		R	4.14 %	+0.3 %
8		Objective-C	2.61 %	-0.1 %
9		Swift	2.29 %	-0.1 %
10	↑	TypeScript	1.91 %	+0.2 %
11	↓	Matlab	1.74 %	-0.1 %
12		Kotlin	1.62 %	+0.2 %
13	↑↑	Go	1.37 %	+0.2 %
14		VBA	1.27 %	-0.0 %
15	↓↓	Ruby	1.26 %	-0.1 %

Figure 2: PYPL ranking

As per TIOBE, the TIOBE Programming Community index is an indicator of the popularity of programming languages. The index is updated once a month. The ratings are based on the number of skilled engineers world-wide, courses and third party vendors. Popular search engines such as Google, Bing, Yahoo!, Wikipedia, Amazon, YouTube and Baidu are used to calculate the ratings. It is important to note that the TIOBE index is not about the best programming language or the language in which most lines of code have been written.

This is what their top 10 in July 2020 looks like:

Jul 2020	Jul 2019	Change	Programming Language	Ratings	Change
1	2	∧	C	16.45%	+2.24%
2	1	∨	Java	15.10%	+0.04%
3	3		Python	9.09%	-0.17%
4	4		C++	6.21%	-0.49%
5	5		C#	5.25%	+0.88%
6	6		Visual Basic	5.23%	+1.03%
7	7		JavaScript	2.48%	+0.18%
8	20	⋀	R	2.41%	+1.57%
9	8	∨	PHP	1.90%	-0.27%
10	13	∧	Swift	1.43%	+0.31%

Figure 3: TIOBE ranking

If you notice, PYPL and TIOBE indexes share the same working principle i.e. *the more times the language is mentioned, the more popular it is assumed to be.*

Their approaches are a bit different, though.

TIOBE measures the sum of 25 search engine hits – including popular Google, Bing, Yahoo!, Wikipedia, Amazon, YouTube, and Baidu.

PYPL measures how often language tutorials are googled by exploring Google Trends.

RedMonk measures this annually and below is the top 10 list for 2020:

1 JavaScript
2 Python
2 Java
4 PHP
5 C#
6 C++
7 Ruby
7 CSS
9 TypeScript
9 C
11 Swift

Figure 4: RedMonk ranking

RedMonk analyses GitHub volume information with the level of interest on Stack Overflow for each language to create a reliable ranking based on interest in the open source community and the number of developers solving problems while working in the language. One concern with this is that GitHub only represents open source projects, so proprietary projects may not be included with the RedMonk index.

Let us pick one last source.

IEEE (Institute of Electrical and Electronics Engineers) is the world's largest technical professional organization. Its membership has long been composed of engineers, scientists, and allied professionals. These include computer scientists, software developers, information technology professionals, physicists, medical doctors, and many others in addition to IEEE's electrical and electronics engineering core.

IEEE rankings are created by weighting and combining 11 metrics from eight sources — CareerBuilder, GitHub, Google, Hacker News, the IEEE, Reddit, Stack Overflow, and Twitter.

Below is IEEE Spectrum ranking:

Language Ranking: IEEE Spectrum

Rank	Language	Type			Score
1	Python▾	🌐	🖵	◎	100.0
2	Java▾	🌐	▯	🖵	95.3
3	C▾		▯	🖵 ◎	94.6
4	C++▾		▯	🖵 ◎	87.0
5	JavaScript▾	🌐			79.5
6	R▾			🖵	78.6
7	Arduino▾			◎	73.2
8	Go▾	🌐		🖵	73.1
9	Swift▾		▯	🖵	70.5
10	Matlab▾			🖵	68.4

Figure 5: IEEE Spectrum ranking

27

I also looked at some other sources, but the above seem to be the most reliable.

The Winner

The above ranking show the same result: **Python** is a heavyweight, ranked almost universally as No. 1. Java is not far behind.

Python is an interpreted, high-level, general-purpose programming language, which was first released in 1991. This was around the time I started coding (in Microsoft BASIC), but it is only recently that I have come across Python.

Thoughts

Python's biggest strengths are flexibility, rapid development, scalability and excellent performance, but why is Python so popular almost 30 years after release?

While a number of reasons can be attributed to Python's popularity, one of the biggest is that Google adopted Python heavily back in 2006, and they have used it for many platforms and applications since. Google created a vast quantity of guides and tutorials for working with Python. Google continues to add a rising list of documentation, support tools, and provides free publicity for the language.

Python is an *official language* of Google, the others being Java and C++. Google is always sponsoring various Python conferences (PyCon, EuroPython, etc).

This despite *Go* language being developed in Google and released as an open source project in 2007. Go doesn't even figure in any of the top 10 lists. One reason could be that the companies performing the rankings are mixing up the results for Go language and Google Go, which is an app.

So, where exactly is Python used at Google?

- Google App Engine - Python was the language Google App Engine was originally designed for. It allows constructing web applications with Python programming language, using its rich collection of libraries, tools, and frameworks.

- YouTube - It uses Python for different purposes: view video, control templates for website, administer video, access to canonical data, and many more. Python is everywhere at YouTube.

- code.google.com - main website for Google developers.

- open source libraries, such as:

  o Google Data Python Client Library - provides a library and source code that make it easy to access data through Google Data APIs.

  o Google APIs Client Library for Python - small, flexible, and powerful Python client library for accessing Google APIs.

  o Google AdWords API Python Client Library - makes it easier to write Python clients to programmatically access AdWords accounts.

Programmers at Google also use Python for Google build system, many system administration tools, Google internal packaging format, binary data pusher, code review tool, A/Q and testing, and lots of Google App Engine apps.

One final thought: one of the core ideas of this book is help create a development team from scratch. If Python developers are scare or too expensive to hire, my recommendation would be to go for the second on the list, namely, **Java** instead of Pyton as our choice of programming language.

CHAPTER TWO

WORLD'S BEST

RELATIONAL DATABASE

S hort Answer: MySQL

Long Answer

The World's best database management system (DBMS) remains Oracle Database, as it has been for many years now.

The Basics

"What is Oracle? A bunch of people. And all of our products were just ideas in the heads of those people - ideas that people typed into a computer, tested, and that turned out to be the best idea for a database or for a programming language."

--- Larry Ellison

Co-founder and Executive Chairman, Oracle Corporation

"Don't obsess over data as a tool, obsess about the future."

--- Jeff Beaver

Co-founder and Chief Product Officer, Zazzle

A database is an organized collection of data, typically stored electronically in a computer system. A database is usually controlled by a database management system (DBMS).

DBMS software primarily functions as an interface between the end user and the database, simultaneously managing the data, the database engine, and the database schema in order to facilitate the organization and manipulation of data.

Together, the data and the DBMS, along with the applications that are associated with them, are referred to as a *database system*, often shortened to just *database*.

A relational database management system (RDBMS) refers to a collection of programs and capabilities that is designed to enable the user to create, update, and administer a *relational database*, which is characterized by its structuring of data into *logically independent tables*.

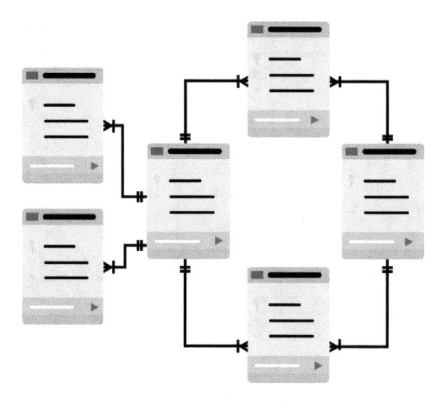

Figure 6: Relational database

In a relational database, data is organized as logically independent tables. Relationships among tables are shown through shared data. The data in one table may reference similar data in other tables, which maintains the integrity of the links among them. This feature is referred to as referential integrity (parent- child relationship) which is an important concept in a relational database system. Operations such as "select" and "join" can be performed on these tables. This is the most widely used system of database organization.

RDBMS base the structure of their data on the ACID (atomicity, consistency, isolation and durability) model to ensure consistency.

The Facts

According to DB-Engines – the best-known source for database management system trends – below are the top 10 databases in July 2020:

Rank			DBMS	Database Model
Jul 2020	Jun 2020	Jul 2019		
1.	1.	1.	Oracle 🔁	Relational, Multi-model 🛈
2.	2.	2.	MySQL 🔁	Relational, Multi-model 🛈
3.	3.	3.	Microsoft SQL Server 🔁	Relational, Multi-model 🛈
4.	4.	4.	PostgreSQL 🔁	Relational, Multi-model 🛈
5.	5.	5.	MongoDB 🔁	Document, Multi-model 🛈
6.	6.	6.	IBM Db2 🔁	Relational, Multi-model 🛈
7.	7.	7.	Elasticsearch 🔁	Search engine, Multi-model 🛈
8.	8.	8.	Redis 🔁	Key-value, Multi-model 🛈
9.	9.	↑ 11.	SQLite 🔁	Relational
10.	10.	10.	Cassandra 🔁	Wide column

Figure 7: DB-Engines ranking

Statista agrees that Oracle is the best:

Ranking of the most popular database management system

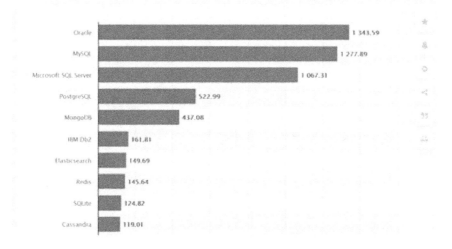

Figure 8: Statista ranking

Datanyze, however, has a different view on this. As per the below research results, Oracle is amongst the top 5, but not the top.

Ranking	Technology	Domains	Market Share
1	Microsoft SQL Server	28,259	18.08%
2	MySQL	24,444	15.64%
3	Microsoft Access	20,079	12.85%
4	Oracle Database (RDBMS)	9,484	6.07%
5	PostgreSQL	7,187	4.60%
6	NoSQL	6,213	3.98%
7	MongoDB	4,901	3.14%
8	Microsoft SSAS Tabular	4,403	2.82%
9	IBM DB2	4,234	2.71%
10	Sybase	3,826	2.45%

Figure 9: Datanyze ranking

The Winner

I could quote analysis upon analysis, but by far, it is clear that **Oracle is the top commercial database** in the world.

I have worked on Oracle and can confirm it is a powerful workhorse. Oracle Database provides the best performance, scalability, reliability, and security for many of the biggest enterprises in the world.

Its enviable list of customers include Panasonic, Mitsubishi, Italian Air Force, Slovak Telecom, IFFCO, Arcor, and DOCOMO.

It appears Oracle database is the first choice of top companies and it does not have any flaws. Except one: it is expensive, especially for small software shops.

Here are the prices from Oracle's official website:

Section I			Prices in USA (Dollar)	
		Oracle Database		
	Named User Plus	Software Update License & Support	Processor License	Software Update License & Support
Database Products				
Oracle Database				
Standard Edition 2	350	77.00	17,500	3,850.00
Enterprise Edition	950	209.00	47,500	10,450.00
Personal Edition	460	101.20		
Mobile Server			23,000	5,060.00
NoSQL Database Enterprise Edition	200	44	10,000	2,200.00
Enterprise Edition Options:				
Multitenant	350	77.00	17,500	3,850.00
Real Application Clusters	460	101.20	23,000	5,060.00
Real Application Clusters One Node	200	44.00	10,000	2,200.00
Active Data Guard	230	50.60	11,500	2,530.00
Partitioning	230	50.60	11,500	2,530.00
Real Application Testing	230	50.60	11,500	2,530.00
Advanced Compression	230	50.60	11,500	2,530.00
Advanced Security	300	66.00	15,000	3,300.00
Label Security	230	50.60	11,500	2,530.00
Database Vault	230	50.60	11,500	2,530.00
OLAP	460	101.20	23,000	5,060.00
TimesTen Application-Tier Database Cache	460	101.20	23,000	5,060.00
Database In-Memory	460	101.20	23,000	5,060.00
Database Enterprise Management				
Diagnostics Pack	150	33.00	7,500	1,650.00
Tuning Pack	100	22.00	5,000	1,100.00
Database Lifecycle Management Pack	240	52.80	12,000	2,640.00
Data Masking and Subsetting Pack	230	50.60	11,500	2,530.00
Cloud Management Pack for Oracle Database	150	33.00	7,500	1,650.00

Figure 10: Oracle prices

Our aim to keep cost as low as possible.

This brings us to the next topper in the list, which is MySQL which began as an open source initiative. Sun acquired MySQL in 2008, only to be itself acquired by Oracle in 2010. Despite this, MySQL still remains open source.

My **recommendation is MySQL** as the database of choice.

DB-Engines, in fact, rated MySQL as the "Database of the Year 2019", which is no mean achievement, considering the competition, especially from its parent Oracle!

Thoughts

Another good database on the list is PostgreSQL (https://www.postgresql.org/), which is consistently amongst the top 5 databases in the world.

If you are paranoid about Oracle turning MySQL into a closed, commercial system, you can pick PostgreSQL.

PostgreSQL has a multitude of features that make it one of the most advanced databases in the world.

As per its website "PostgreSQL is a powerful, open source object-relational database system with over 30 years of active development that has earned it a strong reputation for reliability, feature robustness, and performance."

CHAPTER THREE

WORLD'S BEST

NOSQL DATABASE

Short Answer: MongoDB

Long Answer

NoSQL is an umbrella of database types, each designed for a different use case or data type.

The first challenge for selecting a database is finding the best structure for the data you'll be storing. Sometimes there is a natural fit—for example, airline flight information fits very well in a graph database as this mimics real-life patterns—while long-form web content can usually slot into document databases easily (hence the name).

Choosing structure is about ease of maintenance and optimizing resources. The right structure will fit data logically, deliver data smoothly to applications utilizing it, and easily expand and scale.

The Basics

"In five short years, the MongoDB community has transformed the data management landscape, creating the first compelling alternative to 40 years of relational databases,"

--- Max Schireson

CEO, MongoDB

One of the most fundamental choices to make when developing an pplication is whether to use a SQL or NoSQL database for data storage.

Conventional SQL (i.e. relational) databases, as we have seen in the previous chapter, are designed for reliable transactions and ad hoc queries, the staples of line of business applications. But they are also laden with restrictions—such as rigid schema—that make them less suitable for other kinds of applications.

NoSQL systems store and manage data in ways that allow for high operational speed and great flexibility on the part of the developers.

Many were developed by companies like Google, Amazon, Yahoo, and Facebook that sought better ways to store content or process data for massive websites.

Furthermore, unlike SQL databases, many NoSQL databases can be scaled horizontally across hundreds or thousands of servers.

With SQL databases, all data has an inherent structure. A conventional database like Microsoft SQL Server, MySQL, or Oracle Database uses a schema—a formal definition of how data inserted into the database will be composed. For instance, a given column in a table may be restricted to integers only. As a result, the data recorded in the column will have a high degree of normalization. A SQL database's rigid schema also makes it relatively easy to perform aggregations on the data, for instance by way of joins.

With NoSQL, data can be stored in a schema-less or free-form way. Any data can be stored in any record.

Each NoSQL database tends to have its own syntax for querying and managing the data. CouchDB, for instance, uses requests via JSON, sent via HTTP, to create or retrieve documents from its database. MongoDB sends JSON objects over a binary protocol, by way of a command-line interface or a language library.

Some NoSQL products can use SQL-like syntax to work with data, but only to a limited extent. For example, Apache Cassandra, a column store database, has its own SQL-like language, the Cassandra Query Language or CQL. Some of the CQL syntax is similar to SQL, such as the SELECT or INSERT keywords. But there is no way to perform a JOIN or subquery in Cassandra, and thus the related keywords don't exist in CQL

NoSQL limitations

- No schema: Imposing constraints involves shifting the responsibility from the database to the application developer.

- Eventual consistency: Transaction semantics, which in a SQL system guarantee that all steps in a transaction (e.g. executing a sale and reducing inventory) are either completed or rolled back, are not typically available in NoSQL. For any system where there needs to be a *single source of truth* such as a bank, the NoSQL approach won't work well.

- NoSQL lock-in: While most NoSQL systems are conceptually similar, they implemented differently. Each has its own metaphors and mechanisms for how data is queried and managed. If you decide to migrate from one NoSQL database to another, it can be a major task including re-programming many portions of the application.

Popular NoSQL databases

- MongoDB

    MongoDB is a document store where data is stored in the form of free-form JSON structures or "documents" where the data could be anything from integers to strings to freeform text. There is no need to specify what fields, if any, a document will contain.

    MongoDB supports dynamic schemas, and is free and open source software.

    As per the MongoDB official website, "MongoDB's document model is simple for developers to learn and use, while still providing all the capabilities needed to meet the most complex requirements at any scale. We provide drivers for 10+ languages, and the community has built dozens more."

- Cassandra

Originally developed at Facebook, Cassandra is a decentralized, distributed, column-oriented database engine. It is optimized for clusters, especially those across multiple datacenters, and due to its asynchronous updating and master-less design, Cassandra provides low latency client access. Like MongoDB, it is also free and open source.

Any number of columns (and therefore many different types of data) can be grouped or aggregated as needed for queries or data views.

- Redis

Redis is the most popular and widely-used key-value store implementation. Redis holds its key-value pairings in memory, making their access quick. If data durability is not important (mainly with non-critical data), being able to forego data writes means that this memory-only data boasts incredibly fast performance.

Over the years, APIs have been developed for a wide variety of languages as well, making Redis an easy choice for developers.

- HBase

HBase is a free and open source implementation of Google's BigTable. It is column-oriented database. Some of its popularity and widespread use comes from its close association with Hadoop, as it is part of the Apache project. It facilitates the efficient lookup of sparse, distributed data, which is one of its strongest selling points.

HBase has a number of high profile implementations, including those at LinkedIn, Facebook, and Spotify. With the high numbers of Hadoop installations in existence, and growing, HBase will be a default NoSQL storage solution for many for years to come.

- Neo4j

Neo4j is a graph database management system. The graph database is based on edges acting as relationships, directly relating data instances to one another. Data is represented as a network or graph of entities and their relationships, with each node in the graph a free-form chunk of data.

Neo4j has an open source implementation as well.

Built in Java, Neo4j data can be accessed and updated via the Cypher Query Language,

The Facts

As per DB-Engines, below are the most popular NoSQL databases in the world:

Rank			DBMS	Database Model
Jul 2020	Jun 2020	Jul 2019		
1.	1.	1.	MongoDB	Document, Multi-model
2.	2.	2.	Amazon DynamoDB	Multi-model
3.	3.	↑ 4.	Microsoft Azure Cosmos DB	Multi-model
4.	4.	↓ 3.	Couchbase	Document, Multi-model
5.	5.	5.	CouchDB	Document
6.	6.	↑ 7.	Firebase Realtime Database	Document
7.	7.	↓ 6.	MarkLogic	Multi-model
8.	8.	8.	Realm	Document
9.	9.	↑ 10.	Google Cloud Firestore	Document
10.	10.	↑ 12.	ArangoDB	Multi-model
11.	11.	11.	Google Cloud Datastore	Document
12.	12.	↓ 9.	OrientDB	Multi-model
13.	↑ 14.	13.	RavenDB	Document, Multi-model
14.	↓ 13.	14.	RethinkDB	Document
15.	15.	15.	Cloudant	Document

Figure 11: DB-Engines ranking

But, do we really need to choose between SQL and NoSQL databases? Can't we use both together based on what our use case is?

Fortunately, I am not the only one wondering.

ScaleGrid has performed an excellent survey at DeveloperWeek 2019:

SQL Database Use: 60.48%
NoSQL Database Use: 39.52%

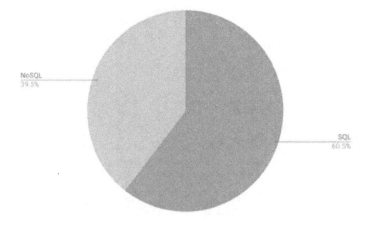

Figure 12: ScaleGrid survey

And here is one: which databases, SQL and NoSQL alike, are most popularly used together.

MySQL + MongoDB: 34.15%
MySQL + PostgreSQL: 9.76%
MongoDB + PostgreSQL: 7.32%
MongoDB + Redis: 7.32%
MySQL + MongoDB + PostgreSQL: 4.88%
MySQL + MongoDB + PostgreSQL + Redis: 4.88%

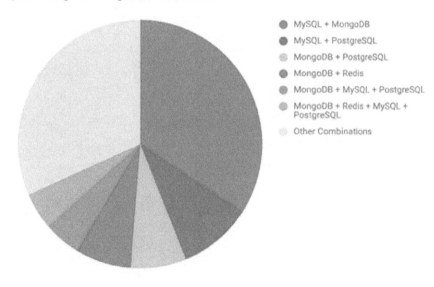

- MySQL + MongoDB
- MySQL + PostgreSQL
- MongoDB + PostgreSQL
- MongoDB + Redis
- MongoDB + MySQL + PostgreSQL
- MongoDB + Redis + MySQL + PostgreSQL
- Other Combinations

Figure 13: ScaleGrid survey

The Winner

So, there we are. **We can use the best of SQL databases and the best of NoSQL databases, by using a combination of MySQL and MongoDB.**

CHAPTER FOUR

WORLD'S BEST

HOSTING

Short **Answer**: Amazon Web Services

Long Answer

Any website needs to be hosted on a good hosting provider so that it is always available to the world.

The Basics

"Overall the web is pretty sloppy, but an online store can't afford to be." ----
Paul Graham

Computer scientist, Co-Founder Y Combinator, author

Since our aim is to look for hosting for an E-commerce site, I am going to ignore excellent static website hosting providers, such as WordPress.

Hosting has come a long way since the early days of the Internet. The current trend is cloud computing.

Amazon Web Services defines cloud computing as "the on-demand delivery of IT resources over the Internet with pay-as-you-go pricing. Instead of buying, owning, and maintaining physical data centers and servers, you can access technology services, such as computing power, storage, and databases, on an as-needed basis from a cloud provider like Amazon Web Services (AWS)."

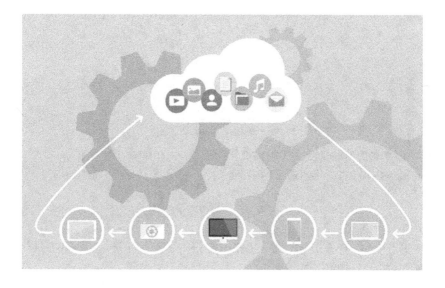

Figure 14: Cloud computing

Its main competitor, Microsoft Azure says, "simply put, cloud computing is the delivery of computing services—including servers, storage, databases, networking, software, analytics, and intelligence—over the Internet ("the cloud") to offer faster innovation, flexible resources, and economies of scale. You typically pay only for cloud services you use, helping lower your operating costs, run your infrastructure more efficiently and scale as your business needs change."

The Facts

How popular is cloud computing?

Statista has the below size of the public cloud computing services from 2009 to 2022 (in billion USD):

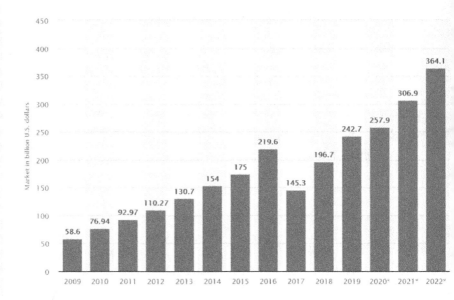

Figure 15: Cloud computing figures

Flexera has found the below:

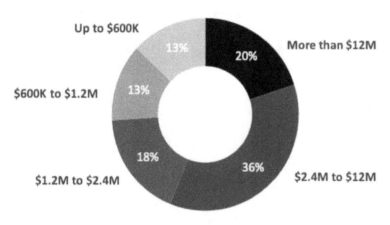

Annual Public Cloud Spend by Enterprises
% of enterprise respondents

Up to $600K — 13%
More than $12M — 20%
$600K to $1.2M — 13%
$1.2M to $2.4M — 18%
$2.4M to $12M — 36%

Figure 16: Public cloud spend figures

Interestingly, they found that cloud computing usage will increase due to to COVID-19:

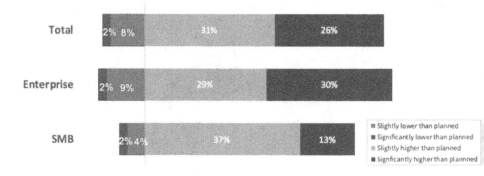

Figure 17: Cloud computing trends

And here are how organizations intend to optimize cloud spend:

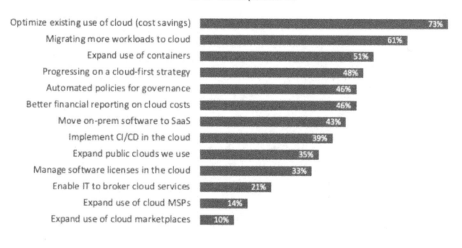

Top Cloud Initiatives for 2020
% of all respondents

Initiative	%
Optimize existing use of cloud (cost savings)	73%
Migrating more workloads to cloud	61%
Expand use of containers	51%
Progressing on a cloud-first strategy	48%
Automated policies for governance	46%
Better financial reporting on cloud costs	46%
Move on-prem software to SaaS	43%
Implement CI/CD in the cloud	39%
Expand public clouds we use	35%
Manage software licenses in the cloud	33%
Enable IT to broker cloud services	21%
Expand use of cloud MSPs	14%
Expand use of cloud marketplaces	10%

Figure 18: Top cloud initiatives

The Winner

Amazon Web Services is our winner. As per its website, Amazon Web Services (AWS) is the world's most comprehensive and broadly adopted cloud platform, offering over 175 fully featured services from data centers globally. Millions of customers—including the fastest-growing startups, largest enterprises, and leading government agencies—are using AWS to lower costs, become more agile, and innovate faster.

The AWS Cloud spans 77 Availability Zones within 24 geographic regions around the world.

AWS is highly customizable, which can also be a drawback since the huge list of options can be confusing.

CHAPTER FIVE

WORLD'S BEST

MESSAGING QUEUE

S **hort Answer**: RabbitMQ

Long Answer

Message queuing allows applications to communicate by sending messages to each other. The message queue provides temporary message storage when the destination program is busy or not connected.

The Basics

The basic concept of a **message queue** is quite simple: there are client applications called *producers* that create messages and deliver them to the message queue. Another application, called *consumer*, connects to the queue and gets the messages to be processed. Messages placed onto the queue are stored until the consumer retrieves them.

Amazon Web Services (which offers a message queuing solution called Amazon Simple Queue Service) describes a message queue as a form of asynchronous service-to-service communication used in serverless and microservices architectures. Messages are stored on the queue until they are processed and deleted. Each message is processed only once, by a single consumer. Message queues can be used to decouple heavyweight processing, to buffer or batch work, and to smooth spiky workloads.

I first used IBM MQ in 2007 (when it was called WebSphere MQ). At that time, there was not as much choice as there is now. For instance, LinkedIn developed Kafka and it was subsequently open sourced in 2011.

IBM MQ was an impressive beast at the time: always reliable and capable of handling high loads. As per IBM MQ's website, below companies rely on MQ:

- 85% of the Fortune 100

- 96 of the top 100 global banks

- 7 of the top 10 manufacturers

- 46 of the Global 100

- 7 of the top 10 global retailers

- 8 of the world's top 10 airlines

- 9 of the top 10 car brands

- 70% of the Fortune Global 500

The Facts

IT Central Station has the below ratings:

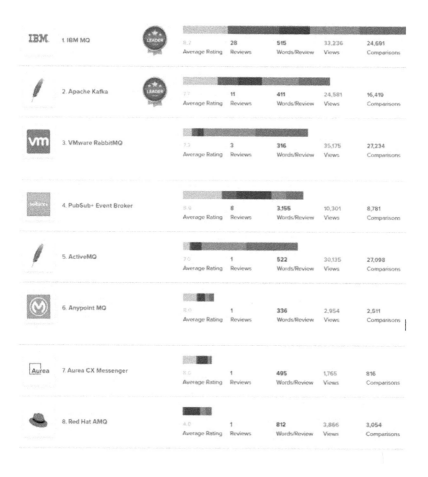

Figure 19: IT Central Station rating

Slant has the following ratings as of July 17, 2020:

BEST MESSAGE QUEUE SERVERS	PRICE	TYPE	LAST UPDATED
RabbitMQ	FREE / PAID	-	Jul 17, 2020
ZeroMQ	FREE / PAID	-	May 7, 2020
NATS	FREE	-	Jul 3, 2020
Kafka	-	monitoring	Mar 11, 2020
Apache Pulsar	FREE	-	Mar 12, 2020
ServiceStack	FREE / PAID	-	Apr 3, 2020
Amazon SQS	-	-	Aug 19, 2019
RocketMQ	-	-	Aug 19, 2019
ActiveMQ	-	-	Oct 19, 2018
Entity Signal	-	-	Jun 14, 2019

Figure 20: Slant ranking

epsagon only compares 3 messaging queue services and concludes that RabbitMQ is the best (lowest score is the winner):

	kafka	RabbitMQ	amazon Kinesis
Ease of Getting Started	0	1	2
Scalability	1	0	2
Maintenance Complexity	2	0	1
Manageability	1.5	1.5	0
Totals	4.5	2.5	5

Figure 21: epsagon ranking

The Winner

For large enterprise applications, IBM MQ is the undisputed gold standard, with more than 25 years in the market.

However, we are now looking for a messaging queue for a standard e-commerce website and lowest costs. For that, we really do not need a messaging queue of the grade of IBM MQ when there are simpler, cheaper, and, indeed, open source options available.

RabbitMQ easily scores over here with offerings of open source and paid versions, and is, therefore our winner. It works with multiple platforms and is constantly rated highly. It is our winner.

RabbitMQ has more than 35,000 production deployments world-wide. It is lightweight and easy to deploy on premises and in the cloud and runs on all major operating systems. It supports most developer platforms, multiple messaging protocols and can be deployed in distributed and federated configurations to meet high-scale, high-availability requirements.

CHAPTER SIX

WORLD'S BEST

JAVASCRIPT FRAMEWORK

FOR

USER INTERFACES

S hort **Answer**: React.js

Long Answer

A JavaScript framework is an application framework written in JavaScript.

A framework is the skeleton of an application. It provides both particular, ready-to-use elements (like libraries and scripts) and a general pattern of how one should use them.

A library is a set of functions that an application can call to perform a particular task.

The Basics

"The kind of programming that C provides will probably remain similar absolutely or slowly decline in usage, but relatively, JavaScript or its variants, or XML, will continue to become more central."

--- Dennis Ritchie

Computer scientist, Creator: C, UNIX, B

Devrant has this hilarious comic on how frequently a new JavaScript framework appears:

WHAT HAPPENS IN ONE MINUTE?

**70,000 Hours of
Netflix watched**

**3 million videos
watched on Snapchat**

**Google is asked
2.4 million questions**

A new JS framework
appears

Figure 22: New JavaScript frameworks

Using a JavaScript frarmework is optional, so why use one? Some of the reasons for me would be the following:

- Efficiency: Programmers have to write less code manually, since the common functions and patterns are already written, waiting to be used. A large part of website features are common (such as displaying search results), so programmers can use the framework for such tasks. They can write only the unique features that are needed on the website.

- Community: Most popular JavaScript frameworks have a large user base. Therefore, extensive documentation, support groups, community blogs, and forums are available.

- Working with larger teams: When working with a larger team, or external developers, using a well-known, well-established framework with existing documentation can reduce the learning curve and make communication between the developers better. Also, it makes hiring the right people easier.

- Generating DOM structures: Frameworks like Angular and React are not generating HTML and then passing it to the browser to have it parsed, instead they generate DOM data structures directly. The Virtual DOM is useful, as they prevent you from re-rendering everything each time you need to update your view.

- JavaScript advantages: Since the JavaScript frameworks are, well, written in JavaScript, all the advantages of JavaScript are present. These include simplicity, speed, interoperability, versatility, frequent updates, and rich interfaces.

The Facts

As per Freecodecamp, below are the Big 5:

1. React

2. Vue.js

3. Angular

4. Ember.js

5. Backbone

Stack Overflow has the below trends chart, but this will keep changing. The below chart was taken in August, 2020:

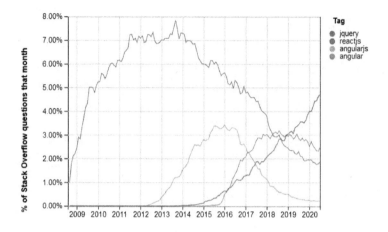

Figure 23: Stack Overflow ranking

Apart from this, Stack Overflow did a developer survey in 2019 with the below results:

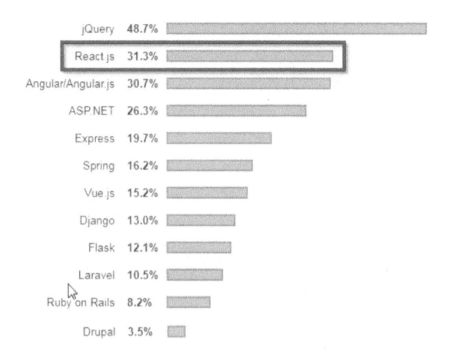

Figure 24: Stack Overflow survey

LambdaTest lists the below:

1. React JS

2. Vue Js

3. Angular JS

4. Ember JS

5. Preact JS

6. Svelte JS

SitePoint lists the below (disclaimer: SitePoints mentions that the "article was created in partnership with Sencha."):

1. Ext JS by Sencha

2. React

3. Angular

4. Vue

5. Ember

6. Svelte

Slant has the below top 10:

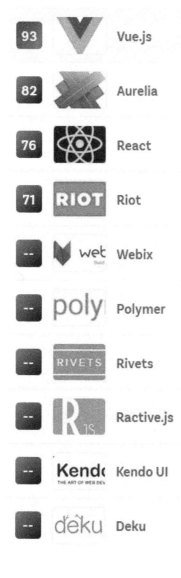

93	Vue.js
82	Aurelia
76	React
71	Riot
--	Webix
--	Polymer
--	Rivets
--	Ractive.js
--	Kendo UI
--	Deku

Figure 25: Slant ranking

classicinformatics has the below top 5:

1. React

2. Vue.js

3. Angular

4. Ember.js

5. Backbone.js

Bestofjs,org has the below top 10 rankings of 2019:

1	**Vue.js** A progressive, incrementally-adoptable framework for building ...	+31.4k ☆
2	**React** A declarative, efficient, and flexible JavaScript library for buildi...	+22.9k ☆
3	**Svelte** Cybernetically enhanced web apps	+20.0k ☆
4	**Angular** One framework. Mobile & desktop.	+12.0k ☆
5	**Omi** Next Front End Framework	+3.8k ☆
6	**Preact** Fast 3kB React alternative with the same modern API. Compone...	+3.8k ☆
7	**Stencil** A Web Component compiler for building fast, reusable UI compo...	+2.5k ☆
8	**dva** React and redux based, lightweight and elm-style framework. (I...	+2.3k ☆
9	**Relay** Relay is a JavaScript framework for building data-driven React a...	+2.1k ☆
10	**Mithril** A JavaScript Framework for Building Brilliant Applications	+1.5k ☆

Figure 26: Bestofjs,org ranking

The Winner

From the above ratings, **React.js** is our choice.

React was developed by Facebook. It was first deployed on Facebook's News Feed in 2011 and later on Instagram in 2012.

React was open-sourced at JSConf US in May 2013.

React Native, which enables native Android, iOS, and UWP development with React, was announced at Facebook's React Conf in February 2015 and open-sourced in March 2015.

CHAPTER SEVEN

WORLD'S BEST

JAVASCRIPT FRAMEWORK

FOR

BACK-END DEVELOPMENT

S hort **Answer:** Express.js

Long Answer

In case you are reading this chapter directly, please read the previous chapter first since a lot of concepts are covered in that.

Backend frameworks are judged by the programming tools, languages, and interfaces they offer. Moreover, developers prefer frameworks that offer pre-configured tools and templates that help them fast track diverse web development tasks.

In other words, an advanced backend framework accelerates the development speed, making the tasks less time consuming for developers. An advanced backend should not be limited to providing a structure, or just a methodology to develop applications, rather it should allow developers to build interoperable platforms that can carry the workload at scale.

The Basics

"JavaScript is not a functional programming language like Lisp or Haskell, but the fact that JavaScript can manipulate functions as objects means that we can use functional programming techniques in JavaScript."

---David Flanagan

Consulting computer programmer, user interface designer, and trainer

"Any app that can be written in JavaScript, will eventually be written in JavaScript."

--- Jeff Atwood

Software developer, author, blogger, and entrepreneur

Although JavaScript was abundantly used for client-side programming, with the introduction of Node.js, new JavaScript frameworks came into existence which could be ideally used for server-side programming.

In 2009, Ryan Dahl, created the server-side JavaScript runtime Node.js using Google's V8 JavaScript engine and C++ libraries. Because of the success that Node.js achieved as a server-side programming language, many frameworks based on Node.js were created. Node was initially released for Linux only.

Node.js is an open-source, portable runtime environment for executing JavaScript code outside of the browser. To run JavaScript on the backend servers, a virtual machine like V8 by Google executes JS in the server so Node is a wrapper around virtual machines like V8 with built-in modules providing rich features through easy to use asynchronous API.

Node.js is available on Microsoft Windows, macOS, Linux, Solaris, FreeBSD, OpenBSD, WebOS, and NonStop OS.

npm (node package manager) is the default package manager for Node.js. It consists of a command line client, and an online database of public and paid-for private packages, called the npm registry. npm is the world's largest Software Registry. The registry contains over 800,000 code packages. Open-source developers use npm to share software.

There are many Node.js frameworks such as Express.js, AdonisJS, Meteor.js, Nest.js and Sails.js.

The Facts

GitHub has the following trends graph:

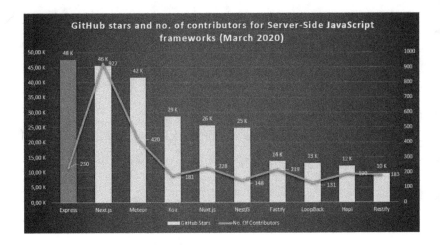

Figure 27: GitHub trends

Hackr lists the below top 10:

1. Hapi.js

2. Express.js

3. Koa.js

4. Sails.js

5. Meteor.js

6. Derby.js

7. Total.js

8. Adonis.js

9. Nest.js

10. LoopBack.js

LambdaTest lists the following:

1. Express.js

2. Next.js

3. Gatsby.js

4. Nuxt.js

CodeBurst lists the following (seems to be same as Lamba but different ranking!):

1. Express.js

2. Next.js

3. Nuxt.js

4. Gatsby.js

NPM Trends has created a graph for most downloads over the last 5 years:

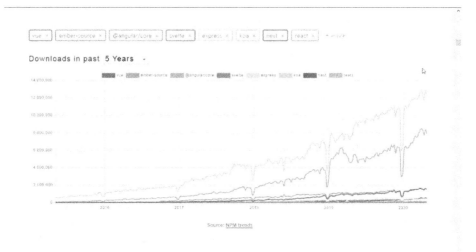

Figure 28: NPM Trends

Express.js is way, way on top.

The Winner

Express.js is a clear winner. Express is a minimal and flexible Node.js web application framework that provides a robust set of features for web and mobile applications. As per its website (https://expressjs.com/), it is a fast, unopinionated, minimalist web framework for Node.js.

Following are some of the core features of Express.js framework:

- Allows to set up middlewares to respond to HTTP Requests.

- Defines a routing table which is used to perform different actions based on HTTP Method and URL.

- Allows to dynamically render HTML Pages based on passing arguments to templates.

- Integrates with "view" rendering engines in order to generate responses by inserting data into templates.

An impressive list of companies use Express.js including Accenture, Mytra, Fox Sports, IBM, and DentiSphere.

Thoughts

Since Express.js is our winner, it might be prudent to keep an eye on koa.js. As per its website (https://koajs.com/) Koa is a new web framework designed by the team behind Express, which aims to be a smaller, more expressive, and more robust foundation for web applications and APIs. By leveraging async functions, Koa allows you to ditch callbacks and greatly increase error-handling. Koa does not bundle any middleware within its core, and it provides an elegant suite of methods that make writing servers fast and enjoyable.

Some key features include:

- Ditched callbacks hell

- Component-based building blocks

- Cascading middlewares

- Quite modular

- Efficient error handling

RAHUL SRINIVASAN

CHAPTER EIGHT

WORLD'S BEST

SOURCE CONTROL TOOL

S hort Answer: Git hosted on GitLab (free version) or GitHub (paid version).

Long Answer

Source control refers to tracking and managing changes to code. This ensures that developers are always working on the right version of source code.

The Basics

"Version control combines procedures and tools to manage different versions of configuration objects that are created during the software process."

--- Roger S. Pressman

Founder and Director of Engineering, EVANNEX

"I did learn fairly early that the best and most effective way to lead is by letting people do things because they want to do them, not because you want them to.

... Let me rephrase that. Much of Linux's success can be attributed to my

own personality flaws: 1) I'm lazy; and 2) I like to get credit for the work of others. "

--- Linus Torvalds

Creator: Linux, Git, Subsurface

Source control systems (also referred as version control systems) are software tools that help a software team manage changes to source code over time. Version control software keeps track of every modification to the code. Programmers can refer earlier versions of the code whenever they want.

Source control is important for maintaining a single source of truth for development teams. Plus, using it helps facilitate collaboration and accelerates release velocity.

That's because it allows multiple developers to work on the same codebase. They can commit and merge code without conflicts. And they can even make edits to shared code, without unknowingly overwriting each other's work.

The first version control software I worked on was the, now discontinued, Microsoft Visual SourceSafe (VSS). This was followed by SVN (with Tortoise SVN), which was miles ahead of VSS. Currently, I am using Microsoft Team Foundation Server.

The Facts

Wikipedia has an amazing comparison of version control software. I would strongly recommend you to browse this:

https://en.wikipedia.org/wiki/Comparison_of_version-control_software

Finances Online performed a compilation of the top 20 version control software of 2020:

1. AWS CodeCommit

2. Team Foundation Server

3. GitHub

4. Jedi VCS

5. IBM Rational Clearcase

6. IBM Rational Synergy

7. Bitbucket

8. Subversion

9. GitLab

10. Git

11. GNU RCS

12. CA HARVEST SCM

13. StarTeam

14. TortoiseSVN

15. Alfresco One

16. ONLYOFFICE

17. Beanstalk

18. HelixCore

19. CVS

20. ArX

For FileCloud, below are the top 5:

1. CVS

2. SVN

3. Git

4. Mercurial

5. Bazaar

Software Testing Help had the below top 10 as of August 1, 2020:

1. Git

2. CVS

3. SVN

4. Mercurial

5. Monotone

6. Bazaar

7. Team Foundation Server

8. Visual Studio Team Service

9. Perforce Helix Core

10. IBM Rational ClearCase

G2 has the following top 10:

1. Microsoft Team Foundation Server

2. AWS CodeCommit

3. Git

4. Subversion

5. Helix Core

6. FogBugz

7. IBM Rational ClearCase

8. Plastic SCM

9. Mercurial

10. CVS

I did a Google Trends search for the last 5 years:

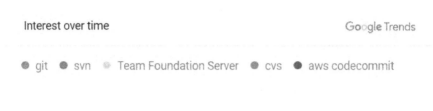

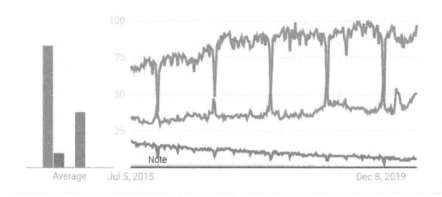

Worldwide. 7/3/15 - 8/3/20. Web Search.

Figure 29: Google Trends of source control tools

As expected, Git is at the top.

The Winner

Before we proceed: what is the difference between Git and GitHub? Git is a version control system which tracks the changes when working with code while GitHub is a Git version control repository hosting service.

Git has been the de-facto leader for years. Git was created by Linus Torvalds, the creator of Linux.

Microsoft bought GitHub for $7.5 billion in 2018.

So, Git is the handler.

Now, look at the best Git hosting service.

For open source projects, **GitHub** is the best. Anyone can browse and download public repositories but only registered users can contribute content to repositories. In the previous chapters, a large number of open-source projects are maintained on GitHub.

Even for private repository hosting, GitHub still remains a good option as the above rankings indicate. Despite buying GitHub, Microsoft has taken no negative steps under the inspirational leadership of CEO Satya Nadella (confession: I have long been a Steve Ballmer critic).

However, if the Microsoft ownership is a cause for concern, the best alternative to GitHub is **GitLab**. If hosting is done ourselves, it is free. Features are also on par with GitHub. If we are looking for hosting to be done by GitLab, **GitHub's paid options** can also be looked into.

THE WORLD'S BEST PROGRAMMER

CHAPTER NINE

WORLD'S BEST

OTHER TOOLS

There a lot of other tools that can be implemented to improve the development process.

I am going to mention a few here.

"The price of reliability is the pursuit of the utmost simplicity. It is a price which the very rich may find hard to pay."

---Sir Charles Antony Richard Hoare

Computer scientist

CI / CD

Continuous integration is a set of practices to establish a consistent and automated way to build, package, and test applications. With consistency in the integration process in place, teams are more likely to commit code changes more frequently, which leads to better collaboration and software quality.

Continuous delivery automates the process of deploying to the required server, such as the UAT server.

CI/CD continuously merges codes and continuously deploys them to production after thorough testing, keeping the code in a ready to release state.

CI/CD creates a fast and effective process of making new releases, whether they be code fixes or new features.

The best tool for automating CI/CD seems to be **Jenkins** (https://www.jenkins.io/).

Jenkins is an open-source tool and is widely used. It will support our selected source control tool (Git).

Payment gateway

Any e-commerce website must have a payment gateway to allow customers to pay online if they choose to do so. Selection of the payment gateway is a business decision. Fortunately, implementation is done by the technical team.

So, here's one important piece of advice: when you implement a payment gateway, ensure that the credit card details are NOT stored on your website, but are stored on the payment gateway site.

The process for this will be as follows:

1. User clicks on "Pay Now" button on e-commerce website.

2. E-commerce site redirects to payment gateway website.

3. User enters credit card details on the payment gateway site.

4. Payment gateway completes the payment.

5. Payment gateway redirects back to the e-commerce site with result of the payment, whether it was successful or not.

6. At the end of the each transaction, day, week, or whichever payment period is agreed with the payment gateway provider, the payments done can be transferred to the e-commerce site's bank account.

Commercials for a payment gateway varies from one to another, but this will not be free.

SSL Certificate

Every e-commerce website must have an SSL Certificate.

SSL is an encryption protocol that secures the communication between the website and the client browsers. This makes it highly challenging for external parties to retrieve any meaningful information from the incoming and outgoing traffic, creating a safe browsing experience for your clients.

To achieve this, an SSL certificate must be bought and installed on the e-commerce website. There are many providers for SSL certificates. All of them have both cheap and expensive options. The EV (Extended Validation) SSL certificate is, for instance, more expensive than a DV (Domain validated) SSL certificate.

When a browser opens a website which has an SSL certificate, it will display a padlock next to the address:

Figure 30: SSL

Clicking on the padlock displays details of the SSL certificate:

Figure 31: SSL Certificate

While choosing an SSL certificate, look for 256-bit encryption. In general, OV (Organization validated certificates) and EV sites today are much safer for users than DV sites, but they are more expensive.

There are many good providers of SSL certificates such as:

- Comodo

- DigiCert

- GeoTrust

- Sectigo

- Symantec

- Thawte

PART II

// Processes //

CHAPTER ONE

SOFTWARE DEVELOPMENT

Agile is the best software development process. Having worked with traditional (waterfall) methodology most of my working life, I will be working backwards to explain how agile methodology is best. Hence, the structure of this chapter will be different from the others.

The Criticism

Waterfall Model was formally introduced by introduced Winston Royce in 1970. Interestingly, Royce presented this model as an example of a flawed, non-working model; which is how the term is generally used in writing about software development—to describe a critical view of a commonly used software development practice

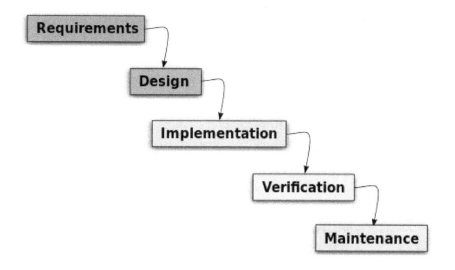

Figure 32: Waterfall model

Critics of this approach say although there isn't a rigorous definition, the key attribute of the so-called "waterfall approach" seems to be extreme inflexibility. In particular:

- Once a phase is completed, its results are frozen. In other words, we cannot return and revise anything based on changing needs or fresh insights.

- The next phase can only commence once the current phase results are completed and approved.

- No working software is produced until late during the life cycle.

- High amounts of risk and uncertainty.

- Not a good model for complex and object-oriented projects.

- Poor model for long and ongoing projects.

- Not suitable for the projects where requirements are at a moderate to high risk of changing.

As per one critic, presumably the waterfall metaphor was suggested by the inability of water to flow uphill. Once you've passed a given point, there's no going back.

Agile

"When to use iterative development? You should use iterative development only on projects that you want to succeed."

--- Martin Fowler

Co-creator, Manifesto for Agile Software Development

In 2001, seventeen software developers (including Martin Fowler) met at a resort in Snowbird, Utah. They were fed up the traditional software methodologies. Together they published the Manifesto for Agile Software Development.

In 2009, a group working with Martin Flower wrote an extension of software development principles, the Software Craftsmanship Manifesto, to guide agile software development according to professional conduct and mastery.

As per the Manifesto for Agile Software Development, the former is to be valued over the latter:

- *Individuals and interactions* over processes and tools

- *Working software* over comprehensive documentation

- *Customer collaboration* over contract negotiation

- *Responding to change* over following a plan

The Agile Principles

To help people to gain a better understanding of what agile software development is all about, the members of the Agile Alliance refined the philosophies captured in their manifesto into a collection of twelve principles. These principles are:

1. Our highest priority is to satisfy the customer through early and continuous delivery of valuable software.

2. Welcome changing requirements, even late in development. Agile processes harness change for the customer's competitive advantage.

3. Deliver working software frequently, from a couple of weeks to a couple of months, with a preference to the shorter time scale.

4. Business people and developers must work together daily throughout the project.

5. Build projects around motivated individuals. Give them the environment and support they need, and trust them to get the job done.

6. The most efficient and effective method of conveying information to and within a development team is face-to-face conversation.

7. Working software is the primary measure of progress.

8. Agile processes promote sustainable development. The sponsors, developers, and users should be able to maintain a constant pace indefinitely.

9. Continuous attention to technical excellence and good design enhances agility.

10. Simplicity - the art of maximizing the amount of work not done - is essential.

11. The best architectures, requirements, and designs emerge from self-organizing teams.

12. At regular intervals, the team reflects on how to become more effective, then tunes and adjusts its behavior accordingly.

Software Craftsmanship

Software craftsmanship is an approach to software development that emphasizes the coding skills of the software developers.

From their official website, below is the manifesto:
"

- Not only working software, but also well-crafted software

- Not only responding to change, but also steadily adding value

- Not only individuals and interactions, but also a community of professionals

- Not only customer collaboration, but also productive partnerships

That is, in pursuit of the items on the left we have found the items on the right to be indispensable."

Agile vs Waterfall

One of the differences between agile software development methods and waterfall is the approach to quality and testing. In the waterfall model, there is always a separate testing phase after a build phase; however, in agile software development testing is completed in the same iteration as programming.

While we "flow" from one phase to another in waterfall methodology, in Agile, testing is part of the development cycle and is done in each iteration.

But above all, Agile is not a methodology but a change in mindset. The iterative approach supports a "product mindset" rather than a "project mindset".

Agile Methodologies

Agile software development methodologies are a group of development techniques or methods that enable software development using various types of iterative development techniques. Many of these methodologies predate the Agile Manifesto. Iterative and incremental development methods can be traced back as early as 1957. The term scrum was introduced in 1986.

Some of the methods are:

- Adaptive software development (ASD)

- Agile modeling

- Agile unified process (AUP)

- Disciplined agile delivery

- Dynamic systems development method

- Extreme programming (XP)

- Feature-driven development (FDD)

- Lean software development

- Lean startup

- Kanban

- Rapid application development (RAD)

- Scrum

- Scrumban

- Scaled Agile Framework - SAFe

And the best is...

For Agile, my recommendation is Scrum with a few practices of XP.

To best understand Scrum, please read this short book from the official Scrum website:

https://www.scrumguides.org/

Written by Scrum co-creators Ken Schwaber and Jeff Sutherland, *The Scrum Guide* is a free, succinct, and complete description of Scrum's roles, events, artifacts, and the rules that bind them together.

Nutcache (https://www.nutcache.com/) has this excellent diagram to explain Scrum:

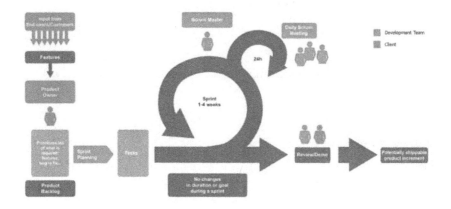

Figure 33: Scrum

While Scrum is a framework, XP is the most specific of the agile frameworks regarding appropriate engineering practices for software development.

One of my favorite practice is pair programming in which 2 programmers sit on the same machine and write the code for the same task. It is especially useful when we have 2 programmers with complementary skills sets or with different experience levels. In such a scenario, not only is better code written but both programmers can learn something from each other.

PART III

// **People** //

CHAPTER ONE

PROGRAMMER QUALITIES

This will be most subjective part of this book. I offer no facts, only my opinion. Different experts will have different perspectives – and some may disagree with me -- but I would be remiss if I did not include what my thoughts on this topic are! I am not including technical skills.

"Integrity is doing the right thing even when no one is watching."

— C.S Lewis, Author

Honesty

For me, honesty and integrity have always been the greatest qualities to have in a person, even if he is not a programmer. Though of us who are experienced programmers, how many times have we accepted a deadline which was unrealistic?

As a manager, I have always appreciated programmers who have been honest to accept that they do not know a concept or that a particular deadline is unachievable. Armed with this knowledge, I can handle the skills gap in the programmer and the client expectations. Each wrong data point adds up to a major wrong decision, handling of which is difficult.

And honesty is not always external. It is internal as well. If you do not recognize gaps in your own knowledge or skills, you will not be able to fill the gaps. As the saying goes, "awareness precedes change".

When you lie, you delude yourself into believing what you're saying. You confuse yourself, confuse others, damage credibility and put yourself at risk.

Desire to constantly learn

With the constant changes in technologies, skills and abilities that a programmer has today will be outdated in a few years. It's imperative to have the love and intent of constantly learning new technologies and improve existing skills.

You need to always be developing new skills to be able to contribute to upcoming projects.

Employers may provide training on company time and dime, but the best developers learn on their own, irrespective of whether it is employer-driven or not.

Communication skills

During my interviews, I do not place much emphasis on communication in the business Lingua Franca English, since I am not looking for my programmers to write essays to our clients!

However, developers must be able to articulate themselves clearly. For instance, it is highly frustrating to ask a dozen questions to acquire a simple status update. During daily stand-up meetings, such developers waste others' time also when it is their turn to speak.

Figure 34: Effective communication

Be a team player

Most commercial software are developed by teams of good programmers. Yes, multi-billion software, such as Facebook and Google, were initially built with the brilliance of individual developers. But now, there are thousands of programmers working on them every day.

You need to be able to deal with people with diverse skills and respond to differences of opinion respectfully.

It is essential to understand that each person succeeds only when the team succeeds overall. This is something that processes such as Scrum also emphasize.

Such programmers also help other programmers get better. They offer teammates help when they are stuck and teach new skills to others.

Be responsible

If you make a commitment, *meet it*.

If you make a promise, *keep it*.

Respecting commitment or deadlines does not mean there can be no possibility of disruption. In case that a commitment cannot be met, ensure that your Team Leader or Manager is aware well before time. A good manager should already have a risk management plan in place to handle such scenarios.

When you write code, you should stand by it. When you *commit* code into your source control tool, you should really *commit*. Committing code should be the equivalent of you signing the code stating that the code is the best possible, error-free code that you could have written and that it meets the user story requirements.

CHAPTER TWO

ON LEADERSHIP

At some point of time, you may make the decision to progress to a leadership role, such as a team leader, a manager, or higher. On the other hand, you may decide to continue as a developer. There is nothing wrong with either approach, depending on your company culture and what you love to do.

Nevertheless please keep in mind that some companies prefer their more experienced (and expensive) developers to take on more leadership responsibilities. If you are not so inclined and your company frowns upon this, you may want to look for outside opportunities.

If you do decide and are given a leadership assignment, first and foremost, congratulations are in order! Someone at a higher position than you believes that you can do more than what you are currently handling. Now, it is up to you to deliver!

If you are reading this chapter without reading the previous one, please read that one first: qualities like honesty are essential leadership qualities as well.

"Management is about persuading people to do things they do not want to do, while leadership is about inspiring people to do things they never thought they could."

--- Steve Jobs

Co-founder of Apple Inc.

Co-creator of the Macintosh, iPod, iPhone, and iPad.

It's not about you

The most important thing to remember is that it's not about you anymore. The moment you walk into a leadership role, you are responsible for your team members.

This may seem a little strange at first since years, even decades, of your life have been spent in working as an individual contributor. Everything you did had been to make yourself shine.

However, now, as a leader, your success is tied to the success of your team. To meet your target, you need to ensure all your team members reach their goals. This may involve some mentoring and supporting your weaker team members.

In any good organization, this should be aligned with the appraisal mechanism i.e. team leader performance ratings are tied to their team's performance.

In the previous sentence, I used the modal verb "should" and not "will" because sometimes it is not so. Some organizations still have incentives and appraisal policies that rate and reward the leader as an individual contributor. Such organizations should not be surprised if the leaders consistently outperform their teams, but the overall business objectives are not being met!

Lead by example

I have always admired leaders who have led from the front, who have rolled-up their sleeves and dug into work themselves, instead of putting up their metaphorical boots on the desk and let their "minions" handle the work.

One of the finest examples of this is Napoleon Bonaparte. Apart from being a phenomenal military strategist, in deadly battles, he would lead the charge himself. As a result of this, only for their le petit corporal, would French soldiers fight stronger, fiercer, and grasp victory from the jaws of defeat. And for no one else.

Also, never assign a task to someone that you are not willing to do yourself.

One more way of looking at leadership is "do what you say and say what you do". For instance, don't look for cost-cutting measures such as reducing your team members' appraisal percentages, but not your own. Or, by denying hardware requests for your team, but requisitioning a snazzy new laptop for yourself.

Passion

Your team will look to you for direction. Therefore, it is important to have positive energy and be passionate about the work at hand and the overall target.

You are the driver of the team, the energy core of the team and you need to ensure that irrespective of your own spirits, you ensure team morale is high and they are focused.

There will definitely be times when the morale of the team will be down. It is your responsibility, as a leader, to keep the spirits from drooping. This is, in many cases, easier said than done.

About the Author

R ahul Srinivasan PMP® has been working since 2001 in the software development field. From 2003, he has been working for the Bird Group. With over 45+ years of experience in India, Bird Group is amongst the largest and most diversified entities within the travel industry.

Rahul Srinivasan holds graduate (BCA) and post graduate (MCA) degrees in computer applications. He also has certifications and certificates in PMP, Certified ScrumMaster, Agile Project Management, Certified Blockchain Expert, Introduction to AI for Managers, and Blockchain and Bitcoin Fundamentals. He has been coding since he was 11.

He can be reached at rahul.software.wbp@gmail.com

EPILOGUE

"So what this builds up to is that in the end we're all here to have fun. We might as well sit down and relax, and enjoy the ride."

--- Linus Torvalds

Creator: Linux, Git, Subsurface

www.ingramcontent.com/pod-product-compliance
Lightning Source LLC
LaVergne TN
LVHW051240050326
832903LV00028B/2497